A TIME TO LOVE
POEMS TO FILL YOUR HEART AND LIFT YOUR SPIRITS

ALEXA HOLBAN

WORD BOTHY

Copyright © 2024 by Word Bothy Ltd.

ISBN: 978-1-913926-34-2 (hbk)

ISBN: 978-1-913926-35-9 (pbk)

ISBN: 978-1-913926-33-5 (ebk)

All rights reserved. No part of this book may be reproduced in any form or by any electronic or mechanical means, including information storage and retrieval systems, without written permission from the author, except for the use of brief quotations in a book review.

For Stu
my man for all seasons

and for Ethan
my little boy with a very big heart

Dear Reader,

May these poems bring you comfort, inspiration, and peace.

On the days when love seems hard to find, may these poems remind you that love is everywhere; you are never alone.

And on the days when you feel enveloped by love, may these poems help you surrender even deeper into your bliss.

Whatever it is you seek, may the wisdom within these poems guide you well.

CONTENTS

Easy to forget	9
Love is always there	11
Never alone	13
One life	15
The grand gestures	17
Don't save time on love	19
Bad relationships	21
As simple as that	23
Your people	25
That kind of day	27
It takes wisdom	29
You can't hold on	31
A growing heart	33
Being human	35
Some goodbyes	37
Holding	39
Love is slow	41
No way of knowing	43
It takes grace	45
New possibilities	47
Fleeting love	49
The dark places	51
Moments of possibility	53
Choose yourself	55
Many places	57
Better left unsaid	59
Letting go	61
I hope you know	63
Keep trying	65
The power of words	67
Living with grief	69
The quietness of a full heart	71

Don't abandon yourself	73
The heart is needed	75
Birds of a feather	77
The magic of connection	79
Light and dark	81
The strong softness of the heart	83
Little things	85
A place beyond	87
Belonging	89
A kind word	91
After you've been hurt	93
All love	95
Ancient wisdom	97
Seeing differently	99
No guarantees	101
The difficult things to say	103
Never a waste of time	105
The ways of the heart	107
There is a place	109
Kindness all the way	111
All there is	113
The gift	115
Some places	117
Dare to let go	119
The paradoxes you carry	121
Love is always there	123
Sometimes all it takes	125
The invisible ones	127
Most love	129
Let it all in	131
The fierce tenderness of the heart	133
Just love	135
Author's note	137
A gift for you	139
About the author	141
Also by Alexa Holban	143

EASY TO FORGET

It is easy to forget
that love is all that matters,
in the end.
It is easy to get caught up
in the drama of everyday life,
the rat-race and the promotions
that push love out of your mind–
temporarily, you tell yourself.
It is easy to forget
amidst all that noise
that love is like a plant;
it needs careful tending
if it is to survive.
It is easy to forget,
because everything
happens so fast
in our fast-paced world,
and love is slow and tender.

It is easy to forget,
but love is all that matters,
in the end.
Do your best to remember.

LOVE IS ALWAYS THERE

Not all fairy tales
lead to happy ever afters;
not all lovers
are there to stay.
Yet even if bad timings
and other disasters
break up a delicate bond,
love is always there, my friend;
love is always there.
Don't grieve too long
for the paths not taken–
no one knows
where they may have led.
Look for the love
that lay at the foundation,
for it is there, my friend;
always there.
Despite everything

that went on,
despite the sadness
and the hurt,
love is always there.

NEVER ALONE

You are never alone,
even if there is nobody
by your side.
You always have
the sunrise as your companion,
the breeze caressing your cheek,
the sky to watch over you.
You are never alone
because there are forests
longing for your visits
and waves eager for your embrace.
Human company fills your heart,
but how can you be alone,
even without it,
when you are part of this world,
a vital piece of a bigger whole
that rejoices
at your every awakening?
You are never alone, dear heart,

so stop behaving as if you were.
Fill your being
with everything that surrounds you
and let the loneliness lift,
for it has no place
in your deeply connected life.

ONE LIFE

It takes heart to understand
the value of life.
The mind doesn't get it.
What is one life among billions?
Yet the heart
sees the invisible tendrils
that bind one life to another
across time and space,
and the ripple effects,
so difficult to predict
yet more certain than anything,
that loss of life has
on everyone who was
touched by it.
The heart sees:
one life is never just one life.
It is many lives,
all entangled

in the invisible magic of love
and the expectation
of a future together,
which may or may not come.

THE GRAND GESTURES

The grand gestures of devotion
are not the ones that truly matter
in the long run.
The romantic dinner in Paris
with all its glittering trimmings
won't measure up
to the peaceful gathering
of tiny thoughtful gestures
that bind two people together
as the years go by.
There are no entrancing stories
about making your loved one smile
on a tough day,
but those short moments matter more,
in ways that cannot be explained,
than the dazzling romantic gestures
that are too extravagant to last.
Don't get swept up by the hype
of a new beginning;

notice what happens
in-between the grand gestures.
That will tell you
if there is enough to build on–
an edifice of small,
almost imperceptible acts of love,
stretching into the possibility
of a happy ever after.

DON'T SAVE TIME ON LOVE

Don't save time on love, dear heart,
to put more into your work jar,
or into the strict fitness regime
you are holding yourself to.
Save time on other things–
like saying "yes" to commitments
you'd rather say "no" to–
but not on love.
Because the truth is
that those who love you
will make do
with as little time
as you will give them.
But love will erode,
hard to notice at first,
yet more and more each day,
until there will be
too little of it left
to stem the tide of resentment

coming your way.
Don't save time on love, dear heart.
Be generous,
and you will feel the difference
in time.

BAD RELATIONSHIPS

Bad relationships
are our most important teachers.
They show us what we were willing
to put up with
before we learned
to say "enough"–
all the ways
we twisted ourselves in knots
to fit into the smallness
of someone else's capacity
to love.
It doesn't feel great,
looking back,
but that's because
we grow from those relationships
the most,
often without realizing.
And looking back confronts us
with the frightened version

of our younger self,
terrified of losing love
that was not worth having,
instead of the love we grew into,
the kind that feels good
without making us
feel small.

AS SIMPLE AS THAT

Sometimes, all it takes
to make up
is the touch of a hand,
or a kind word spoken gently,
for both of you to drop your shields
and look–
really look–
at the other.
It is worth trying,
because if there is willingness
on both sides
to reconnect,
it could be as simple as that.
It won't work every time,
but sometimes is enough
for love to grow stronger
day by day.

YOUR PEOPLE

They hold you tight, your people,
close to their chest,
where you can feel their warmth,
and their nurturing whispers
help your body relax.
They are always with you,
willing you on to keep going
when the going feels hardest
and all you want
is to sink to the ground,
defeated.
Take your troubles to them.
They will understand your pain,
because collectively,
they know how much it hurts;
their compassion
will make the pain lighter to bear.
They hold you tight, your people.

Remember their presence in your life.
You are never alone,
even when it feels like you are.

THAT KIND OF DAY

Some days, you dislike everyone.
It is a "dislike everyone" kind of day,
for reasons unknown.
You are still worthy of love,
and if you remember that,
then it will be easier,
on the days that are good for you,
to be kind to the person
who seems to dislike everyone,
and to remember that they are still
worthy of love,
and that they are a good person,
deep down,
just someone who is having
a "dislike everyone" kind of day,
for reasons unknown.

IT TAKES WISDOM

It takes wisdom to understand
that life is fragile,
and that moments of togetherness
are far more precious
than making progress
on your never-ending to-do list.
It takes wisdom to recognize
the people who truly belong
in your life,
and to let go of those who don't
without blame or resentment,
simply with the quiet knowing
that it is time to say goodbye.
It takes wisdom to look inwards
and learn to love
the dark places you find
without attempting
to disown or improve
your flawed inner beauty.

It takes wisdom, and time,
and as you go through life
experiencing all it has to offer,
your heart will open ever wider
to the gentle balm of this wisdom,
quietly whispering to you
to remember
what truly matters.

YOU CAN'T HOLD ON

You can't hold on to love
that wants to move on
to a new horizon.
All you can do
is to keep the bitterness
out of your goodbye,
and the doubts
out of your memories
of the love that was there.
Let your heart know it is safe.
The sky is not falling,
despite the darkness.
Better days are coming,
even if today
feels insurmountable.
Let your heart know
it is strong,
and it is getting stronger
every time it dares

to open itself up to love,
despite the hurt in its past.
Because one day
you will find love
that wants to stay,
and it will feel good to know
that there is a chance of forever,
even if today,
darkness reigns supreme.

A GROWING HEART

When you are born,
you have a tiny heart,
and you are worried of overloading it,
because you think
it can only take so much.
And then you start growing,
and people bully and betray you,
and your heart starts hurting.
But it can take the pain,
and it grows.
Then you experience your first heartbreak
and your heart grows bigger,
and then more hurt comes,
and more heartbreak.
Bigger and bigger your heart grows,
and as your hair starts turning white,
your heart keeps growing,
until one day, you realize

that your heart is as big
as all the universes put together,
and that it can hold everything.
Everything.

BEING HUMAN

It is tough being human some days.
It is tough to co-exist
with all your longings,
your fears and regrets,
while navigating day-to-day life
in all its unpredictable messiness.
It is tough to hold
so many parts of yourself at once,
and give them a voice
amidst the noise of your becoming.
It is tough to embrace
your ever-present multiplicity,
yet appear to hold it together
despite all the ways
you are falling apart.
Forgive yourself, dear heart;
you are complicated.
And if you look around,

really look,
you will see
that this is part of being human–
complex and conflicted and tender
all in one.

SOME GOODBYES

Some goodbyes
leave us empty and broken,
as if parts of ourselves
have been taken away
and we will never be whole again.
Grief envelops us
like a dark cloud,
and we forget
that the delicate rays of the sun
can warm us back to life.
Yet even in the depths of our sorrow,
there is light.
We must adapt to a new way
of sharing our tenderness,
but the bridge is there, dear heart;
always there.
Do not forget
the tenderness of your heart
and allow the dark clouds

to take over.
Remember that the love that was there
is still there.
You must simply find
new ways of letting it flow,
because no goodbye can withstand
the fierce tenderness
of an open heart.

HOLDING

The safety of being held
is one of the earliest sensations
we have as babies–
that caring enclosure,
our body contained by another.
Don't underestimate
the miracle of holding someone
when they are
at their most vulnerable.
You are giving them
the strength
to know that they are safe
and will not be abandoned
for showing their raw wounds
to another.
Holding–
such a compassionate act,
and in many ways,
so radical.

LOVE IS SLOW

Don't try to rush love, dear heart.
Love is slow.
The delicate bonds of the heart
need time to form, to connect,
to test their unbreakability.
Love likes to take
the scenic route,
so different from the rest
of our goal-oriented lives.
Love has a timing of its own,
careful and tender,
meandering through
this memory and that,
until the tiny seeds
sown a long time ago
start to sprout and grow
into the light.
Don't try to rush love, dear heart.
Trust that the slowness

in which it emerged
will allow it to endure
across time and space,
like a fine wine
that only gets more exquisite
with time.
Don't try to rush love.

NO WAY OF KNOWING

There is no way of knowing
which way
the bonds of the heart
will take you;
no guarantees anyone offers
are written in stone.
We grow and change;
saying goodbye is
something we must learn
to embrace.
But don't let
the lack of knowing
make you doubt
your commitment
to love now,
while the moment
is ripe with possibility.
Let the fragility of life

motivate you to love more, not less.
Because these moments are all we can truly count on; make yours count.

IT TAKES GRACE

It takes grace to love another
exactly as they are,
not wishing away the parts
that do not neatly fit in
with your own desires.
It takes grace to stay together
on the bad days,
the ones when you are tempted
to run into the wilderness,
because togetherness
feels too stifling to bear.
It takes grace to forgive
harsh words spoken in anger
instead of retaliating in kind,
and to come back to the table
again and again,
even though staying away
would be so much easier.
It takes grace, on both sides,

for a relationship to flourish
beyond the passion
of new beginnings.
And if you find
such grace in your life,
and in your heart,
know that you are
one of the lucky few
and that every moment
of grace matters.

NEW POSSIBILITIES

To embrace the silence of aloneness,
or to put up with the noise
of togetherness–
that is the question.
Entering aloneness
feels like ripping
myself in half,
but my nerves are frayed
by the noise of togetherness.
To embrace the silence of aloneness,
or to put up with the noise
of togetherness–
there are no answers,
only questions,
and old habits
that need to die out
for new possibilities
to emerge.

FLEETING LOVE

Fleeting love leaves seeds in its wake
that we may only discover years later,
when they sprout into the fullness
of longer-lasting relationships.
Fleeting love is necessary
for some of us,
to show us what is possible,
and also what we cannot live without.
It is not in vain.
It is a sacred initiation
into a future that will never be,
a road not taken
that we may often wonder about
in later years,
and may romanticize
when the drudgery of reality
threatens to engulf
our whimsical wings.

Fleeting love matters,
more than we realize;
it is a sacred milestone
on the path to our becoming.

THE DARK PLACES

The dark places within you
need even more of your love
than the rest.
The bits you don't want
to tell anyone about–
those places hold within them
so much light,
so much spirit,
a warrior who is waiting
to be discovered
and to bring their medicine
into the world.
Love them
into revealing their light,
their spirit,
their truth,
and your wholeness.
For you deserve to be whole,

light and darkness together,
as one.

MOMENTS OF POSSIBILITY

There are moments of possibility
in every interaction.
Moments when there is an opening
to say the things
that are difficult to say,
yet necessary to hear;
uncomfortable truths
that require courage
to be brought to the surface,
or perhaps loving words
that have never been spoken out loud
and may never be,
unless you dare to say them
before it is too late.
Seize these moments
as often as you can.
Speak with courage,
and trust that if the words

need to be spoken,
they will be heard
the way they are intended.
There is no time like the present;
speak the words.

CHOOSE YOURSELF

Choosing someone else
over yourself
never works out in the long run.
Choose yourself,
forever and always;
you will have
so much love to give.
Others will see
what it means to thrive
rather than survive
and they will choose
themselves too,
because they will know
that shining brightly
is the only truthful way
to be selfless.

MANY PLACES

There are many places
that can hold your heart–
not just people,
but your work, your pets,
the sight of a rainbow
appearing after a storm.
Broaden the scope
of what love is,
and you will see–
even on the loneliest of days,
your heart still has places to go,
where you can find
that inner warmth
that keeps the pain of heartbreak away.
There are many places
that can hold your heart,
and the more you open yourself up
to the heart's infinite possibilities,
the more resilient you will be

when the unexpected
throws you a curveball
and the frostiness of isolation
threatens to take over.
There are many places
that can hold your heart;
keep looking.

BETTER LEFT UNSAID

Some things
are better left unsaid;
the truth takes time
to reveal itself.
Whatever harsh words
are on your lips,
don't spill them out
into the world just yet.
Perhaps they will take
a gentler form soon.
Sit with your feelings;
give them time to mature
and see if they change.
For now, wait.
Some things
are better left unsaid.

LETTING GO

Love that makes you
tense up in fear
is not worth holding onto,
no matter how bright
the moments of joy are
that you have been able to rescue
from the wreckage.
Don't gaslight yourself
the way you have been gaslit
by others.
Allow truth to finally
take up center stage.
There are shiny glimmers of possibility
in every relationship,
but they are not enough,
if the foundation is rotten.
Put your arms around yourself
and give yourself a hug.

Better days are coming.
For now, focus on the gift
of letting go, and healing,
and finding yourself anew.

I HOPE YOU KNOW

I hope you know how much light
you bring into the world.
I hope you know how much poorer
everyone's life would be
without your presence,
your smile, your voice.
I hope you know
that every word you speak,
every story you tell,
makes an indelible mark
on those around you;
that your uniqueness
will be remembered
for a long time after you are gone.
I hope you know
that your flaws
are like water in the desert
for those who need to discover
the brightness

showing through the cracks.
I hope you know your worth,
dear heart,
so you don't allow others
to tarnish your light.
I hope you know.

KEEP TRYING

Not all of us are good
at making friends.
Our instinct is to keep ourselves
to ourselves.
We are safer that way, we think;
but we are also lonely.
Not always, but sometimes,
and if you try to befriend us
in a way that does not scare us off
too much,
you may be surprised
at how welcoming we can be.
But you have to take
that first step, my friend,
because there is an invisible forcefield
holding us back from reaching out.
And when we
go back into our cave,
because we must,

to breathe out the overwhelm
of our togetherness,
keep trying,
after a while,
to coax us back out.
Don't stop trying,
but gently,
because as impenetrable
as it may seem,
our heart is like a butterfly;
it frightens easily.
But if you keep trying,
we will,
like a wild animal
getting used to eating
out of a human's hand,
learn to trust.

THE POWER OF WORDS

Your words have such power.
They have the power
to lift someone up
from the pits of despair,
conjuring up new possibilities
that set the imagination alight
with wonder and curiosity
at what might be.
They also have the power
to hurt another soul,
to make them feel
less than nothing,
until they gather up the strength
to undo the knots
you have cast upon their being.
Which one will you choose?
Your words carry across
oceans and continents;
they can reach strangers

just as easily
as lifelong friends.
How will you use
this extraordinary power?
Choose well.

LIVING WITH GRIEF

Grief is not something
you can get over,
however hard you try.
You are a new person now;
someone who has loved and lost.
Yet grief is not the enemy.
If you stop resisting
its agonizing balm,
grief will allow your heart
to open wider
than you ever thought possible.
And as you grow
in your capacity to hold
both love and pain
within your heart,
you will one day realize
how much grief
has enriched your life

through its much-needed reminder
that life is fragile
and every moment
of togetherness counts.

THE QUIETNESS OF A FULL HEART

There are no awards for love.
There is no parade celebrating you
when you love someone
in just the way they need to be loved,
and hold them in just the way
they need to be held.
There are no awards
for being at their side
through good days and bad.
In this world of glittering trophies,
there is no recognition
for all these extraordinary
acts of heroism;
only the quietness of a full heart
that illuminates you from within.
So counter-cultural,
this power
we have within us,
which we either

open ourselves up to or not,
because there is no incentive
other than the love itself,
and the way it permeates
our whole being.
What a feeling,
what a way to be,
what a gift.

DON'T ABANDON YOURSELF

Don't abandon yourself
in the hope of winning over
someone else.
If you are the one
putting in all the effort,
what are you actually winning?
That promise of togetherness
won't last,
not beyond the point
you start expressing
your anger.
Because that is the moment
when the illusion shatters,
and it becomes obvious
you were the only one
in the game
all along.
You don't have to take
these abysmal terms.

The ball is in your court
even while you are waiting
for a response,
because silence is plenty of words
to speak the painful truth
you need to hear
to be free.

THE HEART IS NEEDED

The heart is needed
to make life happy.
Other things matter too–
money and recognition
and a sense of mastery over your life–
but having these
will not quench
your soul's longing
if the heart is missing.
It is the vital ingredient
that brings everything else together.
It is easy to forget,
and then wonder
at your lack of happiness
when you have so much.
The heart is needed, my friend.
The heart is needed.

BIRDS OF A FEATHER

It is rare to find birds of a feather
as you make your way through life.
When you do,
be generous with your time.
Open yourself up
to the gifts of togetherness;
kind words and smiles
go a long way
to keep the bond strong.
It is rare to find birds of a feather,
and when you do,
make sure you treat them with care,
so they know they have found
a welcoming other
to witness their journey
through the ups and downs
of life.

THE MAGIC OF CONNECTION

The magic of connection
is like a balm
that carefully sweeps over
your wounds
and reminds your body
how to heal itself.
The magic of connection
is not limited by time and space.
It binds us together
across continents,
through delicate tendrils
stretching across
the vast expanse of existence.
At times, it may seem
to fade and recede
into the background of our lives,
barely a whisper,
as our attention
is caught elsewhere.

But at the slightest remembering
it springs back to life,
vibrant and ever-present,
opening our heart wider
while offering
the delicate balm of its embrace.
Trust the magic of connection
to heal
even the most painful of goodbyes,
because the delicate tendrils of love
will always be there,
stretching out into eternity.

LIGHT AND DARK

You are neither good nor bad.
You are both light and dark,
as multi-faceted as the night sky.
There is evil in you,
just as there is goodness,
both part of being human,
two sides of the same coin.
Yet your dark parts
need your love the most.
And when they feel loved,
they melt into the whole of who you are
and join the circle of animals
in the unique song
of your multiplicity.

THE STRONG SOFTNESS OF THE HEART

Physically, the heart
is so much stronger
than we give it credit for.
It pumps blood around the body
and keeps us alive
every minute of the day.
But emotionally, the heart
can be as soft as a butterfly,
delicately flapping its wings
while hoping
to find love and acceptance
in the hearts of others.
A paradox:
strength on the one hand,
softness on the other.
And because the heart
is so delicate emotionally,
we often don't realize
how much pain it can take.

We treat it like an invalid
when it is a warrior,
always at our side,
with the delicate demeanor
of a butterfly.

LITTLE THINGS

It is the little things
that matter the most,
in both good ways and bad.
The little gestures of thoughtfulness,
the throwaway comments we make,
all add up over time,
giving rise to a tsunami
of wonder or despair
from which there is no return.
It is easy to dismiss their significance
on rational grounds,
but the bonds of the heart
are strengthened or weakened
by the little things
we do to each other
and barely notice.

A PLACE BEYOND

There is a part of the journey
from feeling worthless
to discovering your own worth,
where being asked
to sacrifice your dreams
for someone else
gives rise to uncontrollable rage.
How dare you ask me
to put myself second again,
after I have worked so hard
to figure out who I am?
That rage is valid; you come first.
But there is a place beyond that,
where it is okay to give of yourself,
because you can,
and have enough for everyone,
including yourself.

BELONGING

Forgive yourself for wanting to belong
when you cannot find the right place
to make a home for your soul.
Not all places will welcome
the circle of animals
resting within your chest.
When you find yourself
in a place that fills you
with equal parts
of dread and longing,
trust that there will be arms
big enough to hold you
even when you point
to the cracks in the wall
and the leaky faucet.
You belong.
Keep asking where.

A KIND WORD

A kind word makes all the difference
in being able to see the world anew.
It sometimes only takes a whisper
to bring a battered soul
back from the edge;
a gentle promise of peaceful bonding,
so different from the wars
of before.
A kind word is a gift you can offer
to weary travelers at your door.
Invite them in,
make them feel welcome,
and smile upon their high-strung souls.
You will see miracles aplenty
with such simple medicine as a kind word;
some of us need it like water,
while making our way
through the desert.

AFTER YOU'VE BEEN HURT

It is hard to trust again
after you've been hurt;
to dare open your heart
once more
knowing how bad
the damage can get
if things don't work out.
You are right to be guarded
in the beginning.
Trust takes time to build;
there is no rush.
But don't keep your heart
shielded forever.
Allow for the possibility
of a new beginning.
The warmth trickling back
into your heart
may be exactly what you need
to heal.

ALL LOVE

Most love does not end
in happy ever-after.
It ends in blame and recrimination,
in love songs about toxic relationships
and bad break-ups.
Yet why is the happy ever-after
the only acceptable standard?
All love teaches us
something about ourselves,
about what we need and don't need,
about our impossible longings
and the parts of us
that are easy to love.
All love plants seeds
of understanding,
memories that gather in meaning
as the years pass,
about who we were
and who we are becoming.

All love teaches us to let go,
however grudgingly,
of our fairy tale visions of the future,
and learn to embrace
the love that was there all along,
waiting to be acknowledged
in its imperfect flawlessness
for all the ways it opened our heart.

ANCIENT WISDOM

If we saw how helpless
we all are
to the will of the gods,
perhaps we would be gentler
with one another for our failings.
The ancient people knew
that when someone
is acting out of character,
it is because the gods are upon them
and there is nothing the person can do
but obey.
Why have we chosen to forget,
in our sophistication,
such simple wisdom?
Our free-will arrogance
makes us ignorant
of the storms raging upon our being
from the beyond.
And so when the tendrils

of the invisible bind us,
turning us into their puppets,
we accuse and blame each other,
instead of seeing the power of the gods
behind it all.

SEEING DIFFERENTLY

It is amazing how different
a place can look
when you see it
from a calm frame of mind.
No resistance,
plenty of patience,
laughing things off
when they don't go to plan.
Like seeing the world
with new eyes,
you suddenly realize
how much was available
that you didn't notice before.
Forgive yourself;
redemption is open to you.
Put it close to your chest,
and remember
the kindness of strangers.

It is always there,
if you look the right way.

NO GUARANTEES

There are no guarantees
that the person you love
will love you back,
or even treat you
with a bare minimum
of humanity.
But if your heart
wants to love them anyway,
allow yourself this love;
just not their presence.
Not everyone we love
is worthy of our gift;
that is sad,
but in some ways,
the love is not about them anyway.
It is about the light within you
that is seeing the light within them,
buried beneath the surface
of their behavior.

It is the light
you were loving all along,
and that light will glow brighter
the more you allow yourself to love,
and let them go,
because you will always have their light,
the one buried within,
to remember them by.

THE DIFFICULT THINGS TO SAY

The difficult things to say
are the ones that need
to be said most urgently.
Not in a flash of anger,
but calmly, lovingly,
at a time when the other
is ready to hear
difficult truths spoken gently.
As tempting as it is
to pretend that everything is fine,
the pressure of unspoken truths
builds and builds,
ready to erupt
at the most inopportune moment;
that is the danger.
Don't turn your truth
into volcanic lava.
Allow it to flow like water,
gentle and cleansing,

responsive to the other's needs.
The difficult things to say
are worth saying;
the solid foundation
of your togetherness
depends on it.

NEVER A WASTE OF TIME

Opening your heart to another
is never a waste of time,
even if you end up drifting apart.
The heart needs to open,
to learn what togetherness feels like,
and what letting go feels like too.
It needs to know
that both are part
of the rich tapestry of life,
and that it can survive
the pain of separation,
because more togetherness
is coming.
The heart must remember
to stay open and welcoming
when there is a chance to find
delicate moments of encounter
that may or may not repeat
with the same person

but will happen again and again,
as the wind blows this way and that,
bringing with it
the promise of new adventures
in the journey of being human.

THE WAYS OF THE HEART

The ways of the heart
are too simple
for our complicated minds
to grasp.
The heart does not care
about status or ambition,
or about carving out
a place in the world.
It only wants warmth
and comfort and safety.
The ways of the heart
seem child-like,
yet the heart reaches further
than the mind ever will,
like water penetrating
where the sharp axe cannot.
The ways of the heart
are too simple
for our complicated minds to grasp.

And sometimes,
you have to trust your heart
to take you into the unknown,
where you will feel safe
and loved and welcomed
for no reason at all.

THERE IS A PLACE

There is a place inside my heart
where hope lives
despite all the contrary evidence
that life is putting before me.
Whether real or not,
it gives me strength
when all the fight has gone out of me
and I am ready to crumble.
I go to that place often,
and there is always
a welcoming fire burning
despite everything,
or because of everything.
Nothing has been able
to extinguish it.
My last refuge,
when everything falls apart;
there is still hope

inside my heart
somewhere.

KINDNESS ALL THE WAY

Look at yourself with kindness
when you look;
what good would harsh words do?
It is easy to be
your own worst enemy,
but the power lies
in being your best friend.
Look at yourself with kindness
when you look;
kindness all the way.

ALL THERE IS

Love is all there is, anyway;
everything else is simply noise.
We tend to forget that
when we wrestle
with the miracles
that life brings before us
instead of recognizing
their sacred role
in our becoming.
But now and again,
we wake up from slumber
and notice the gentle wisdom
holding us in its embrace.
Love is all there is.

THE GIFT

There is always a gift
in even the deepest of sorrows.
You may have to dig deep
to find it,
because the gift likes to hide sometimes
from the inquisitive nature of the mind.
But find it you will
if you search with your heart
knowing it is there,
like a forgotten treasure
at the bottom of an old box.
There is always a gift
in even the deepest of sorrows,
and if you trust
from the beginning
that the gift is there,
then the pain will be easier to bear,
because you will know

that the gift will be waiting for you
like an old friend
to open your heart
and see.

SOME PLACES

Some places wrap us
so tightly in their embrace
that no matter how worn down
we are from our travels,
we can't help but feel
cozy and warm
as we drift off to a peaceful sleep
full of nurturing dreams.
Some places allow us to be,
simply be,
and seem not to notice
our shortcomings,
letting us grow into ourselves
at our own pace,
as if having the freedom
to grow into ourselves
was the most natural thing
in the world.
Some places are so full

of love and acceptance
that it is easy
to take their kindness for granted,
and drift off to wilder adventures
filled with heartache and pain,
until one day we remember
what it felt like
to simply be held and accepted,
and we return to the warmth
and the gentle healing
that only some places offer.

DARE TO LET GO

Dare to let go
of the lover who scorned you,
dare to rejoice
at the coming of spring.
You cannot build
your foundation on crumbs;
better days are coming.
Can you feel the shift in the air?
Dare to let new love
flow in through the window
and allow the emerging sunlight
to dry your tears.
Better days are coming.
Trust in the wisdom of life
and let go.

THE PARADOXES YOU CARRY

Some days you do not have the words
to express the complexity of your feelings.
Some days you experience
both hatred and gratitude,
both awe and disgust,
towards the same person
in the same breath,
and wonder how your heart
can hold all these contradictions
without exploding into a million pieces
from the strain of the paradoxes you carry.
Some days you are a child
unable to speak,
yet able to hold so much
of what it is to be human,
while sobbing on your knees
on the bathroom floor,
under the inscrutable gaze
of a newly found god.

LOVE IS ALWAYS THERE

Love is always there
in the background of your life,
like music playing louder one day
and quieter the next.
Can you hear its gentle tune?
Love comes upon you
in the most unexpected ways,
trusting it will be welcomed
with open arms,
no matter how inconvenient
its arrival.
Do not question its wild ways
of making itself known.
It likes to hide from your mind,
peeking at you
from this place and that,
to catch you unawares.
Open yourself up to its mystery,

even when you can barely hear it
above the noise of the world.
Love is always there,
waiting for you to open your heart
and see.

SOMETIMES ALL IT TAKES

Sometimes all it takes
is a kind word spoken gently
to open your heart
and let love in.
Sometimes all it takes
is the touch of a hand
to let you feel the longing
inside your chest
for another person's breath
upon your skin.
Sometimes all it takes
is a smile
to let you see the world anew,
as if you were a different person
instead of the embittered warrior
still fighting
yesterday's wars.
Sometimes all it takes

is one moment
that changes everything.
Everything.

THE INVISIBLE ONES

They speak to you every day,
the invisible ones,
hiding in a ray of sunshine,
the breeze caressing your face,
a ladybird landing on your hand.
They stay with you always,
a quiet presence
at the back of your mind,
guiding your thoughts from afar.
They are even closer to you
in death than in life,
for they have nowhere else to be,
no business to attend to,
other than walking by your side
day by day,
quietly and steadfastly,
until the day you join them
and become the gentle breeze
weaving its way through the world.

MOST LOVE

Most love does not start
with passionate embraces
upon first encounter.
These make great moments in a film,
melting our heart
with their sweeping romanticism.
But in real life,
most love starts slowly, quietly,
through fleeting moments
that are easily forgotten at first.
They may only gather meaning
once love is in full bloom
and we can see those moments
as sacred milestones
ripe with significance.
Most love does not
make itself known;
it takes us by surprise
when it eventually reveals itself,

like a magician distracting us
when there is magic to perform.
We were not prepared,
because we were looking
for the movie-worthy moments,
which made us miss
the breadcrumbs of longing
that love scattered on our path.
Most love builds slowly, quietly,
like a magic trick waiting
for the big reveal.

LET IT ALL IN

Open your heart
to the sadness,
open your heart to the pain.
Let it all in,
because when you do,
you are also letting in
the other side–
the delight, the ecstasy,
at anything and everything.
The tiny raindrops on your window
and the flower peeking
through the cracks in the concrete
become magical manifestations
of the mystery of life–
the ugly and the beautiful,
the grotesque and the sublime,
every color of the rainbow
lighting up inside your heart,

and what an explosion of joy
you experience
when you let it all in.

THE FIERCE TENDERNESS OF THE HEART

The fierce tenderness
of the heart
knows no bounds;
it can withstand
the most painful of goodbyes
and the longest of absences.
It does not care
about what is reasonable;
it only knows
the magic of invisible bonds
connecting kindred spirits
across time and space.
The fierce tenderness of the heart
lingers long after
the reality of togetherness
has ceased to exist.
The breeze
gently brushing your cheek,
a ray of sunshine,

the waves of the sea,
become new ways
for memories to hold you
in their embrace,
allowing the fierce tenderness
of the heart
to thrive,
unbounded
by the world of form.

JUST LOVE

The whole of life
is about taking off
the veils of distortion
that are clouding your vision
and learning to see
the world anew,
veil after veil,
until your vision
is fully restored
and all you can see
is the light amidst the darkness.
It's all about seeing, dear heart–
seeing what is there,
instead of all the things
that are missing.
Seeing the miracles that arise
out of the disaster;
the gifts that are born
out of tragedy.

It is about seeing
the rainbow following a storm,
bypassing your complicated mind,
and realizing
how simple it all is
underneath the surface.
Just love.
That is all.
Just love.

AUTHOR'S NOTE

Dear Reader,

Thank you for spending some time immersed in these poems. I hope they have brought you comfort and insight.

Passing on words of wisdom to one another is how we have survived as a species. I hope my words have given you what you needed.

Please consider gifting this book to any loved ones who may draw comfort from it too.

I would also like to ask you for a small favor.

Reviews are the best way to spread the word about this book. If you have enjoyed reading these poems, it would mean a lot to me if you could leave an online review.

Even if you only write a sentence or two, it will help.

Thank you!

A GIFT FOR YOU

As a thank you for giving these poems space within your life, here is a gift for you, dear reader.

www.alexaholban.com/gift

ABOUT THE AUTHOR

Alexa Holban is the pen name of non-fiction author Alexa Ispas.

Alexa turned to poetry as a way of healing from trauma, when her seemingly healthy son Ethan abruptly went into end-stage heart failure at age two-and-a-half.

Ethan was diagnosed with "dilated cardiomyopathy," a condition characterized by an enlarged heart, and put on the urgent heart transplant list.

Several harrowing years followed, which included spending a year in hospital by Ethan's side, not knowing whether he would live or die, waiting for the gift that eventually saved his life.

During this time, Alexa used poetry as a way of transforming her life experiences into powerful wisdom to share with anyone who needs it.

Alexa believes that by providing clarity and powerful imagery, poetry can bring light into even the darkest of places, allowing us to turn our difficult feelings into nourishment for the soul.

May this book bring light and clarity into your own life, dear reader. And if it does, please feel free to get in touch: mail@alexaholban.com

ALSO BY ALEXA HOLBAN

A Time to Play

A Time to Shine

A Time to Heal

A Time to Speak

A Time to Dream

A Time to Trust

For more information, please go to:

www.alexaholban.com

www.ingramcontent.com/pod-product-compliance
Lightning Source LLC
Chambersburg PA
CBHW030039100526
44590CB00011B/271